HARMONY IS FUN

BOOK 3

Maureen Cox
Kate Hewson

First published 2001
by **Subject Publications**
  Bishops Court
  Wallace Road
  Broadstone
  Dorset BH18 8NF

ISBN 1 898771 16 2

Printed by Pardy & Son (Printers) Ltd.,
Parkside, Ringwood, Hampshire, BH24 3SF
Tel: +44 (0)1425 471433
Fax: +44 (0)1425 478923

Authors' note

This is the final book in a series of three books. In the first two books you met six musical family members - **Mother, Father, Daughter, Cousin, Grandmother** and **Grandfather**. You harmonised melodies using their **root position** and **first and second inversion chords**. Now you will also meet one **third inversion chord**.

 In this book we shall introduce you to another family member, **Uncle**. You will meet the families of **E Major** and **A♭ Major**. Their **Minor Relatives** will be shown in an expanded **Magic Circle of Keys**. You will also find a variety of useful chord progressions with suggested fingering.

With the additional **rules of harmony** introduced in this book, you will be able to compose and play a greater variety of chords and harmonise melodies using some exciting **new rhythms**. Once again you will discover that Harmony is Fun.

Acknowledgements

We are grateful to Subject Publications for inviting us to write this third book and thereby giving us the opportunity to continue the enjoyable task of conveying to others the pleasure and excitement of harmony.

We are especially grateful to Alison Hounsome for her careful study of our manuscript and her constructive comments. If there are ambiguities or errors in this book, we the authors are entirely responsible.

Maureen Cox & Kate Hewson

CONTENTS

Meet the Family

In Book 2 you met six members of the
musical family. Let's look at them again.

The **Inner Family** Consists of

 **Mother**
the **Tonic**
Chord I

Daughter
the **Subdominant**
Chord IV

 **Father**
the **Dominant**
Chord V

Father can also add a 7th to his chord.

He is then
the **Dominant 7th**
Chord V^7

You also met three relatives.

Cousin is
the **Supertonic**
Chord II

Grandfather is
the **Mediant**
Chord III

Grandmother is
the **Submediant**
Chord VI

More Next-door Neighbours

In Book 2 you met seven **Major** families with their **Relative Minors**. You will now meet some more families.

 **E Major** with 4 sharps: F, C, G & D

and its Relative Minor **C♯ Minor**

 **A♭ Major** with 4 flats: B, E, A & D

and its Relative Minor **F Minor**

The **Magic Circle of Keys** has grown.

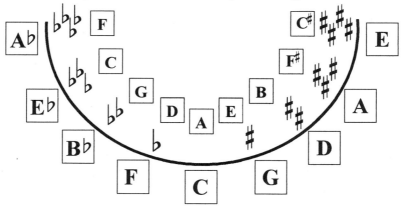

The complete **Circle of Keys** is on page 60.

Getting to Know the New Keys

Draw *with* key signatures:

Daughter's chord IV in the **E Major** Family →

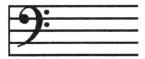 **Mother's chord I** in the ← **A♭ Major** Family.

Father's chord V in the **A♭ Major** Family →

 **Chord I** in the ← **E Major** Family

Chord IV in the **A♭ Major** Family →

Let's play those chords! **I** tonic, **IV** subdominant and **V** dominant.

Dominant 7th Chord

Here are **dominant** and **dominant 7th** chords of **E Major** in root position.

Draw **dominant** and **dominant 7th** chords of the following keys in the same way.

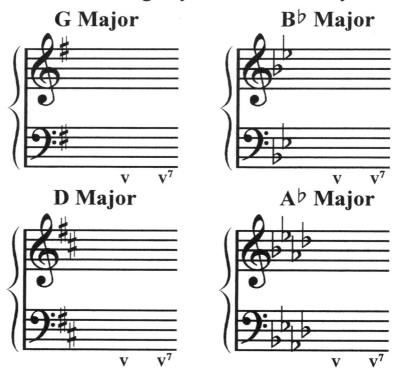

G Major   B♭ Major

D Major   A♭ Major

Play each pair of chords and listen to their different sounds.

Harmony with the Inner Family

Here are two tunes for you to play in your new keys. They use the three chords of the **Inner family** plus Father's **dominant 7th**.

Remember the Relatives

Play these two chords in **A Major**.

Cousin's Chord II may sometimes be used instead of **Daughter's Chord IV**.

Grandfather's Chord III can sometimes take the place of **Father's Chord V.**

Draw and play both chords in **B♭ Major**.

Grandmother's Chord VI can sometimes be used in place of **Mother's Chord I.**

Draw and play both chords in **A♭ Major**.

Using the Relatives

Chords **II**, **III** and **VI** are **minor** chords. If you use them occasionally in a **major** key they add variety to your harmonies.
Play these three pieces.
Listen to the chords.

Do **not** use chord **II**, **III** or **VI** in the last cadence of a piece. Use members of the Inner Family for that 'final' feel.

Chord VII

You have met every chord in our musical families except **Chord VII**. Below we have drawn all the chords in **F Major**. Play them and listen to their sounds.

| I | II | III | IV | V | VI | **VII** | I |

Chord VII (a diminished chord) is neither major nor minor, making it difficult to use. Think of it as an **Uncle** who very rarely visits.

Draw all the chords for **C Major**.

| I | II | III | IV | V | VI | VII | I |

Play the chords and listen to their sounds.

The Leading Note

Although chord VII is difficult to use, the **7th note** of a scale is *very* useful. Known as the **Leading Note**, it *leads up* to the tonic.

Important Rules:
1. **Never** double the Leading Note.
2. If the **Dominant** Chord is followed by the **Tonic** Chord, the **Leading Note** must move **upwards** ➔ by **one semitone**.

Play the following examples:-

Now draw your own chords for **F Major** and **D Major**. Play and listen to your chords.

A Quick Look Back

The E Major Family has __ sharps and its
Relative Minor is __ Minor.

The A♭ Major Family has __ flats and its
Relative Minor is __ Minor.

The Inner Family of chords.

chord **I**
tonic

chord __
subdominant

chord __
dominant

chord __
_____

Four Other Family Members.

chord __
supertonic

chord __
_____

chord __
_____

chord __
_____

Sometimes Cousin (**II**) replaces daughter (**IV**),
Grandfather ( ) replaces father ( ), and
Grandmother ( ) replaces mother ( ).
Uncle chord ( ) is neither major nor minor.
The Leading Note of a scale is the __th note.

Chords In Major Keys

Root position chords can be drawn on **any note** of the scale. Play all these chords for two major scales drawn in four different ways.

4 notes in the right hand

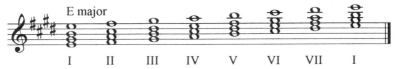

4 notes in the left hand

3 notes in the right hand and 1 in the left

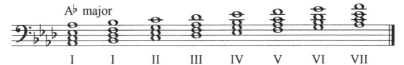

2 notes in the right hand and 2 in the left

When **1st inversion chords** are formed on **every degree** of the scale, the **3rd** is now at the bottom.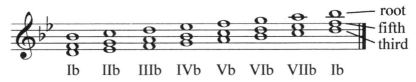

Play these 1st inversion chords in **B♭ Major**.

Ib   IIb   IIIb   IVb   Vb   VIb   VIIb   Ib

Draw and play all the first inversion chords for **D Major** in the *left hand only.*

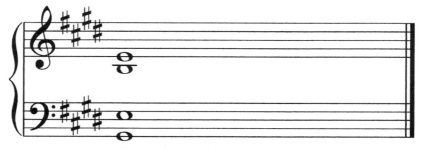

Ib   IIb   IIIb   IVb   Vb   VIb   VIIb   Ib

Draw and play all the first inversion chords for **E Major** with *two notes in each clef.* Remember to put the 3rd at the bottom.

Ib   IIb   IIIb   IVb   Vb   VIb   VIIb

Second inversion chords are mainly formed on the notes of **Inner Family**.

Put the **5th** of the chord at the bottom.

Play these three second inversion chords in **A♭ Major**.

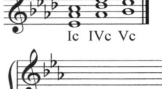

Complete and play these 2nd inversion chords of **E♭ Major**.

Play these **Inner Family triads** for **C Major** in root position, first and second inversions.

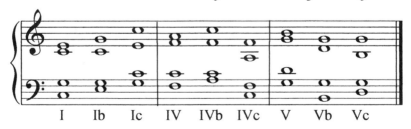

Now play the same chords, this time shared between two hands. Try other major keys.

The **dominant 7th chord (V7)** has **three** possible **inversions** because of its extra note.

From the previous pages you saw that **chord V** can have only two inversions.

You build a third inversion in the same way as you build 1st and 2nd inversions and you distinguish a third inversion with the letter **d**.

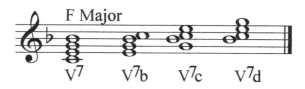

F Major

V^7 V^7b V^7c V^7d

Some rules when using the _third inversion_ of the dominant 7th:

1. Always put the 7th in the bass.

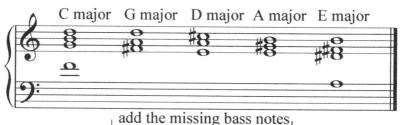

C major G major D major A major E major

add the missing bass notes

2. Do not double the 3rd or 7th notes.

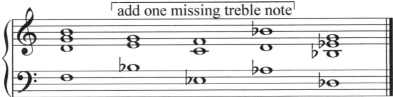

add one missing treble note

C major   F major   B♭ major   E♭ major   A♭ major

3. Double the root if you omit the 5th note.

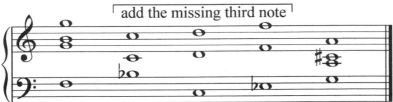

add the missing third note

C major   F major   G major   B♭ major   D major

4. Never omit the 7th note because the result would no longer be a V^7 chord.

V^{7}b   Vb

Note that the 3rd inversion of Father's Dominant 7th Chord usually *resolves* to the first inversion of Mother's Tonic Chord, the 7th falling one step and the 3rd rising one step.

F Major

V^{7}d → Ib

Harmonising a Melody

Play this melody in the key of **E♭ Major**.

Now play the harmonised melody. Put the
missing chord names in the empty boxes.

Harmonic Minor Scales

Play this harmonic minor scale and notice that the **7**th note has been raised by one semitone ascending *and* descending.

E Harmonic Minor

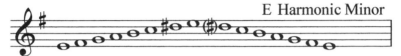

Over to you

Write the scale of **D Harmonic Minor** ascending and descending with key signature. Remember to raise the 7th note.

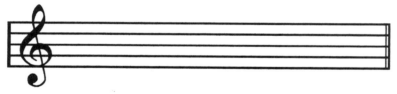

Now write the key signature and scale of **G Harmonic Minor** ascending and descending.

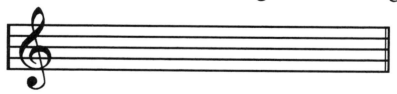

Play all the scales on this page. You will find other Minor Scales on pages 52-54.

Minor Keys

Chords in minor keys are usually formed on the notes of the **Harmonic** Minor scale.

In **root position** you should build chords on notes **I, IV, V** and **VI**. *

The following are in the key of **D Minor**.

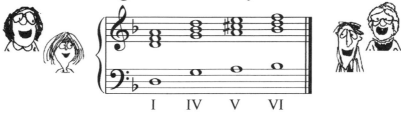

Play the chords. Notice that the 7th note of the scale has been raised one semitone.

Now draw chords in the key of **E Minor**.

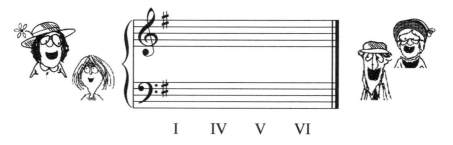

---

* Chords built on notes **II**, **III** and **VII** of Harmonic Minor Scales are scarcely ever used in harmony.

In Minor Keys you can use six **first inversion chords**. The only *exception* is **Grandfather's Mediant, III.** Play all the chords on this page.

Add the ***bottom note*** to complete each of these first inversion chords in **A Minor.** Remember the raised 7th.

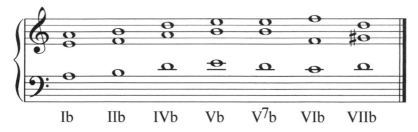

Ib   IIb   IVb   Vb   V⁷b   VIb   VIIb

Second inversion chords in Minor Keys are mainly formed on the notes of the **Inner Family.** Add the ***top note*** in the treble clef to complete these chords in **B Minor.**

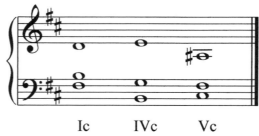

Ic   IVc   Vc

Answers. *A minor:* C, D, F, G#, G#, A, B. *B minor:* B, E, F#.

Chords in Minor Keys

Here are melody notes in four different keys with a harmonised version below. Draw in the missing note for the chords marked * to give two notes in each clef.

Play your chords and listen to the sounds.

Melodic Minor Scales

A tune in a minor key usually uses the **Melodic Minor Scale** in which you **raise** the **6th** and **7th** notes when **ascending** and **lower** them again when **descending**.

Here is the scale of **G Melodic Minor** in the treble and bass clefs. Play the scales with separate hands and then hands together.

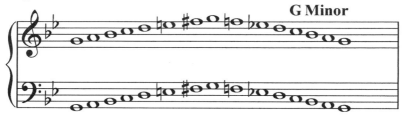

Write the scale of **E Melodic Minor** in both Treble and Bass clef. Play each scale with separate hands and hands together.

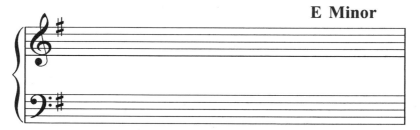

You will find all scales on pages 52-54.

Major or Minor?

Play this piece of music.

Is it written in **D Major** or **B Minor**?

Clues
D Major: its final melody note will probably be **D** with a bass note **D** and Mother's tonic chord **D**.
B Minor: it will probably end with Mother's tonic chord **B**. There may be **A♯**. There may also be **G♯** if the melodic form is used.

Play the following piece. Is it written in **G Major** or **E Minor**?

Using Chords in Minor Keys

Here are chords in the key of **G Minor**. Notice that we have used two notes in the right hand and two in the left hand. Put the names of the chords in the empty boxes.

V ☐ IVc ☐ VII ☐ ☐ VIb ☐ I

Here is a melody in G Minor. Add one 𝅘𝅥. to each named chord to complete the harmony with two notes in each clef.

I IVb Ic VIb VII IVc V V⁷ I I

ᴸɅ qʌI I I ɔI

Check your answers

Missing 𝅘𝅥. notes:
G, E♭, D, E♭, F♯, G, F♯, F♯, D, B♭

Play your harmonised melody.

Doubling the Third

If chord **VI** in a **Minor** key comes before or after chord **V** you may **double** the 3rd instead of the root or 5th. Play these chords.

VI→V   V→VI

Add notes to complete the following chords, two notes in the right hand and two in the left

I   I   I   Ib   IIb   IV   Vb   V^7 Vc   V^{7}d   IVb

Complete this harmonisation. Use the chord numbers to help you. Now play the piece.

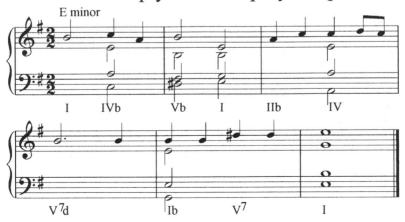

I   IVb   Vb   I   IIb   IV

V^{7}d   Ib   V^7 I

Binding Notes

When writing harmony, the aim is to move as smoothly as possible from note to note. Using a **binding note** helps us to do this. Look at this example in **E Major** where chords **I** and **V** are next to each other.

The binding note, **B**, is the same for both chords. The other notes in the right hand move stepwise, first down then up.

Here is an example, with chords **I** and **IV**. This time **E** is the binding note. The other notes in the right hand move stepwise, first up then down.

 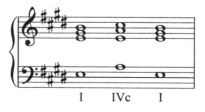

Play all the chords carefully.

Over to you

Complete the chords in the following four major keys. Use a **binding note** to connect the three chords in each sequence.

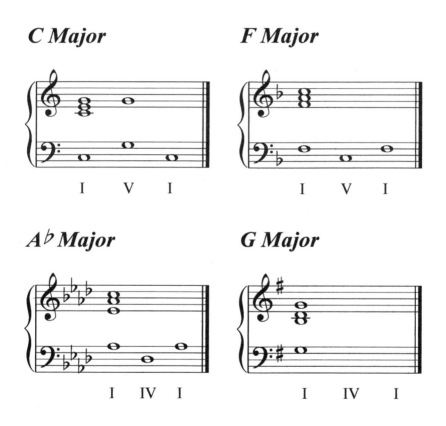

C Major

I V I

F Major

I V I

A♭ Major

I IV I

G Major

I IV I

Play all the chords and resolve to use some binding notes in your harmonisations.

Melodic Decoration

1. Essential Notes

We rarely harmonise every melody note with its own separate chord, except perhaps for hymns and stately tunes such as the National Anthem.

Melody notes that are harmonised but *not with their own separate chords* are called **essential notes**. Here is an example with the essential notes clearly shown.

The note marked **u** is called an **unessential note** because it is *not* from the same chord.

2. Passing Notes

These are **unessential** notes because they do not belong to the harmonised chords.  Nevertheless **passing notes** add a great deal to the melodic decoration.

Passing notes move *step by step* either upwards or downwards. They form a smooth link between harmonised notes.

Play this example and notice the use of block chords. The **p** marks the passing notes.

Now play this example and notice the use of broken chords. Mark the passing notes.

3. Auxiliary Notes

These unessential notes add to the melodic decoration but unlike passing notes they move a step *above or below* a note of the harmony and then *return* to that note.

Play this example. The auxiliary notes have been marked **a**. Notice the use of three-note chords in the left hand. This is another style for you to try.

Mark the six auxiliary notes in this passage. Play it and listen to the variety of chords.

N.B. Ornaments are largely built from auxiliary notes. These can be studied in detail in Theory Is Fun Grade 4.

Over to you

Use this piece of music to practise melodic decoration with unessential notes. Add *one* **passing** note at places marked **p** and *one* **auxiliary** note at places marked **a**.

Play your enriched composition and listen to the effect of the notes you have added.

Modulation – Change of Key

This is changing key *during* a piece of music usually without a change in the key signature. Modulation occurs most easily with families living near each other on the magic circle, i.e. Major and Relative Minor or keys with one sharp or flat more or less than the *home* key.

For example, G Major can most easily modulate to the keys of E Minor, D Major and B Minor, C Major and A Minor.

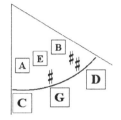

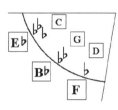

G Minor can most easily modulate to the keys of B♭ Major, C Minor, E♭ Major, D Minor and F Major.

The full magic circle is on page 60.

Complete the following two examples.

home key	*most easily modulates to keys of*				
E♭ Major	____	____	____	____	____
F♯ Minor	____	____	____	____	____

Over to You

The following piece modulates from a major key to its relative minor. The leading note in the new key rises to its tonic to establish the new key.

Decide for yourself

Play this piece. It begins in the key of _____. In bars 8 to 9, the music modulates from _____ to _____. The piece ends in the key of _____.

Helpful Relatives

1. Father's **dominant chord V^7b**
This chord is used for a *strong* perfect cadence in a *major or minor* key because it has **two** notes pulling to resolve. Play these three resolutions. Complete the last one yourself.

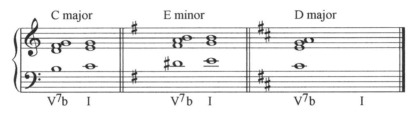

Now play this passage and notice how chord V^7b provides a perfectly natural link as you modulate from D Major to E Minor.

2. Cousin's **chord II**

Try chord II especially if you are modulating to a ***flatter*** key.

Example: modulation from **C Major** to **F Major** using the **D Minor chord II** as a link.

Notice the B♭ and think key signature F major

3. Grandmother's **chord VI**

Try chord VI especially if you are modulating to a ***sharper*** key.

Example: modulation from **C Major** to **G Major** using the **A Minor chord VI** as a link.

Notice the F# and think key signature G major

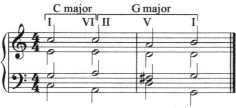

Play all the chords. Notice how chord VI in one key becomes chord II in the new key.

Adding Notes to Chords

Extra notes can enrich the sound of chords. You already know how to draw chord V^7 by adding a seventh to the dominant chord.

Now you can enrich other chords with extra notes by adding sixths, sevenths and ninths.

Add to chord	I	II	III	IV	V	VII
● sixth	●			●		
● seventh	●	●	●			●
● ninth	●				●	

Play and listen carefully to the following examples. Complete the names of the chords in the empty boxes underneath them.

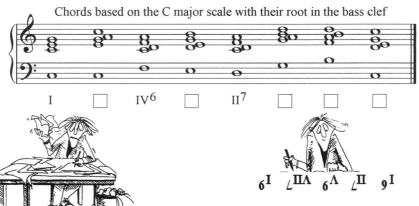

Chords based on the C major scale with their root in the bass clef

I   ☐ IV^6 ☐ II^7 ☐   ☐   ☐

$_6I \quad _7IIA \quad _6A \quad _7II \quad _9I$

page 42

Over to You

Play this piece and listen to the chords enriched with a sixth, seventh or ninth note.

Changing Notes in Chords

The triad **C-F-G** is the 'suspended fourth' chord that likes to resolve to the **C Major** tonic chord **C-E-G**. The triad **G-B-D♯** is an 'augmented fifth' chord.

Play and listen to the following chords.

Have fun changing notes in other chords.

A Quick Recap

Describe each of the following tonic notes as **auxiliary, binding, essential** or **passing**.

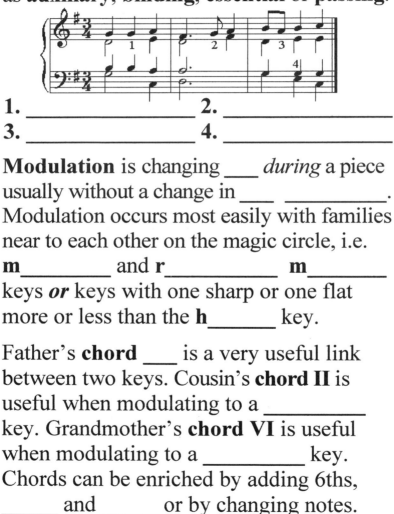

1. _____ 2. _____
3. _____ 4. _____

Modulation is changing ___ *during* a piece usually without a change in ___ _____. Modulation occurs most easily with families near to each other on the magic circle, i.e. **m_____** and **r_____ m_____** keys *or* keys with one sharp or one flat more or less than the **h_____** key.

Father's **chord** ___ is a very useful link between two keys. Cousin's **chord II** is useful when modulating to a _____ key. Grandmother's **chord VI** is useful when modulating to a _____ key. Chords can be enriched by adding 6ths, _____ and _____ or by changing notes.

Experimenting With Rhythm

On the following pages there are some new rhythms for you to enjoy with three harmonised pieces to play and three melodies for you to harmonise and play.

Remember

(1) Father's dominant 7th can resolve onto Mother's tonic chord and Daughter's subdominant chord can lead to Father's chord V or Mother's chord I.

(2) Cousin's chord II may replace Daughter's chord IV, Grandfather's chord III may replace Father's chord V and Grandmother's Chord VI may replace Mother's Chord I.

(3) Do not use chords II, III or VI too often and do not use them in a final cadence. Try to make use of the 1st inversion of Cousin's chord II and 2nd inversions of Mother, Father and Daughter chords.

(4) Double the root or fifth of a chord but only double the third in Chord IIb. Never double the leading note or the seventh note of a dominant chord.

(5) To end a piece use a perfect cadence with Father's chord V or V^7 going home to Mother's tonic chord. If the tonic chord follows the dominant chord, the leading note moves upwards by one semitone.

Oom-Pah Rhythm

Notice the steady rhythm of the left-hand.

Play, sing and enjoy this piece.

Oom-Pah-Pah Rhythm

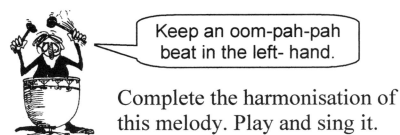

Keep an oom-pah-pah beat in the left- hand.

Complete the harmonisation of this melody. Play and sing it.

Swinging Blues

Twinkle, twinkle little star,
I don't wonder what you are.
Just a ball of white hot gases,
Cooling down to molten masses.

Here is a new rhythm for a well-known tune. Notice the simplicity of the notes in the left-hand as you play this version.

Syncopation

This well-known carol
has been given a
syncopated rhythm.
Keep the left-hand
simple when you harmonise this tune.

Off-beat Rhythm

Play this piece. Note that the left-hand has the chords and the right-hand single notes.

Music does not have to be complicated to be effective. Rhythm is so important.

Over to You

Harmonise this tune in an **offbeat** style.
Use three- and four-note chords in the bass
clef. Their numbers are given to help you.

Major Scales
and their Relative Minors

Remember in harmonic minor
scales to raise the seventh note
ascending *and* descending.

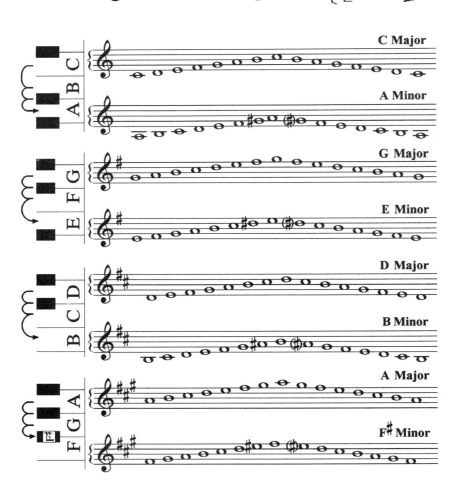

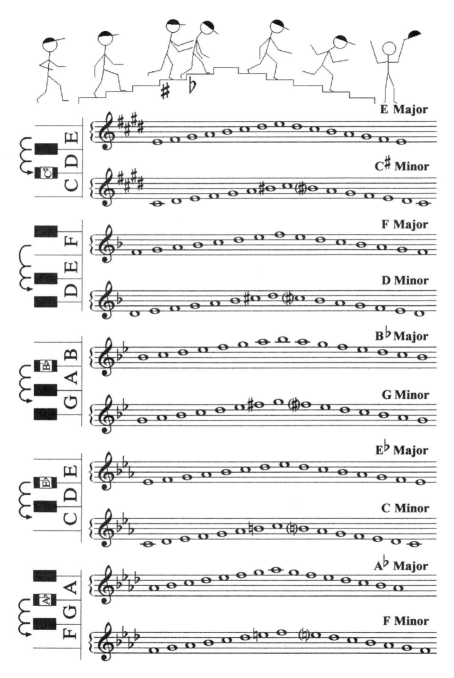

Melodic Minor Scales

Remember in a melodic minor scale to raise the 6th and 7th notes ascending and to lower them again when descending.

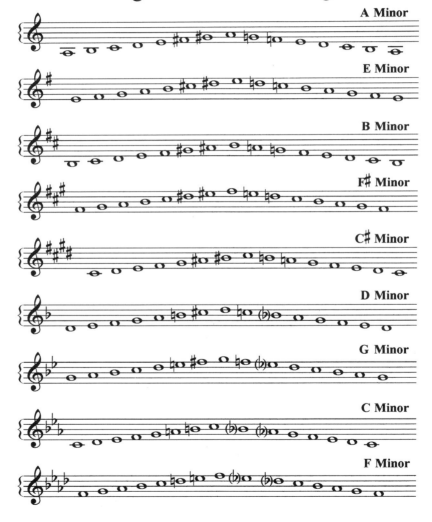

Chords in Major Keys

Match each chord with its family member.

Chords in Minor Keys

Match each chord with its family member.

Fingering Chord Sequences

Some chords are easier to play than others. Here are some useful chord sequences that are fairly easy to finger and play.

I-IV-V-I

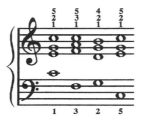

chord I	chord IV

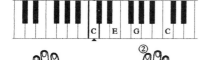

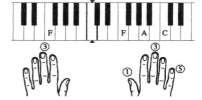

chord V	chord I

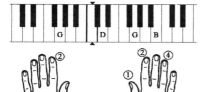

Useful Chord Progressions

Consistent fingering makes playing easier. Try the following fingering and chord sequences in other major and minor keys.

The 7th note of chord V^7 as an essential note.

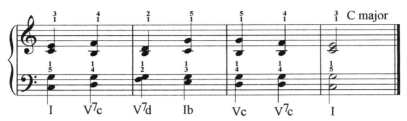

The 7th note of chord V^7 as a passing note.

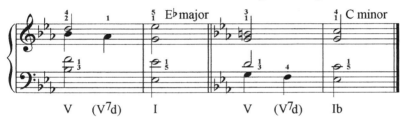

Practise harmonising scales in different keys.
Try using enriched chords (see page 42).
Finger and play the following examples.

The Magic Circle of Keys

The **Major** families on the **outside** of the circle have the same key signature as their **Minor** relatives on the **inside** of the circle.

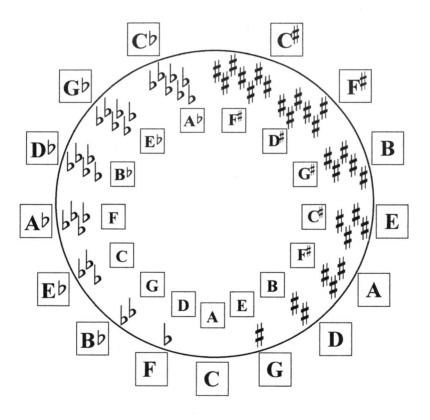

List of terms

auxiliary note   unessential notes in a chord sequence that move by step, up or down, then back again

binding note   a note common to two or more consecutive chords

broken chord   the notes of a chord played one after the other

cadence   the half or full close of a musical phrase or section

      imperfect   any chord going to chord V suggesting a pause for breath

      perfect   chord V going to chord I with a strong feeling of ending

      plagal   chord IV going to chord I with a weaker feeling of ending

chord   two or more notes that are played together

      in close position   the notes of a chord are as close together as possible

      in open position   the notes of a chord are spread widely

chord I (or Ia)   tonic chord in root position

      Ib   tonic chord in first inversion

      Ic   tonic chord in second inversion

      a   letter to show root position

      b, c, d   letters to show first, second and third inversions

II	supertonic chord
III	mediant chord
IV	subdominant chord
V	dominant chord
V⁷	dominant 7th chord
VI	submediant chord
VII	chord formed on the leading note

Vb V⁷b

dominant
[Father]   5th note of a scale and the chord
                    grown from that note: e.g. G and
                    G-B-D in the scale of C Major

dominant 7th   dominant chord with an added
                    7th note: e.g. G-B-D-F
                    in the C Major scale

doubling   the same note (root or 5th and, in a
                    minor key, perhaps 3rd in chord II)
                    used twice in the same chord

essential notes notes from the same
                    chord that are not
                    separately harmonised

first inversion chord with its 3rd note at the bottom
leading note   7th note of a scale and the chord
[Uncle]   grown from that note: e.g. G and
                    G-B♭-D♭ in the A♭ Major scale

mediant   3rd note of a scale and the
[Grandfather]   chord grown from that note:
                    e.g. F♯ and F♯-A-C♯ in the
                    scale of D Major

page 62

modulation	changing key during a piece without a change in the key signature
passing notes	unessential notes in a chord sequence that move by steps *either* up *or* down
resolving	movement of a note or chord to a more satisfying note or chord: e.g. chord V^7 to chord I
root	note from which a chord grows: e.g. C is the root of the tonic chord of C Major
second inversion	chord with its 5th note at the bottom
subdominant [Daughter]	4th note of a scale and the chord grown from that note: e.g. B♭ and B♭-D-F in the F Major scale
submediant [Grandmother]	6th note of a scale and the chord grown from that note: e.g. F♯ and F♯-A-C♯ in the A Major scale
supertonic [Cousin]	2nd note of a scale and the chord grown from that note: e.g. C and C-E♭-G in the B♭ Major scale
triad	a three-note chord: e.g. the tonic triad G-B-D of the G Major scale
tonic [Mother]	1st note of a scale and the chord grown from that note: e.g. E♭ and E♭-G-B♭ in the E♭ Major scale

V^7b I

IVc

THEORY IS FUN GRADE 1

Treble clef, bass clef, notes and letter names. Time names and values; dotted notes, tied notes and rests. Accidentals. Tones and semitones.
Key signatures and scales (C, G, D & F Major).
Degrees of the scale, intervals and tonic triads.
Simple time signatures and bar-lines.
Writing music and answering rhythms.
Musical terms dictionary and list of signs.

ISBN 0-9516940-8-1

THEORY IS FUN GRADE 2

Major key signatures and scales to 3 sharps or 3 flats.
A, D and E minor key signatures and scales.
Degrees of the scale and intervals. Tonic triads and accidentals.
Piano keyboard, tones and semitones.
Simple time signatures. Grouping notes and rests. Triplets.
Two ledger lines below and above the staves.
Writing four-bar rhythms
More musical terms and signs.

ISBN 1-898771-02-2

THEORY IS FUN GRADE 3

Major and minor key signatures to 4 sharps or 4 flats.
Harmonic and melodic minor scales.
Degrees of the scale, intervals and tonic triads.
Simple and compound time signatures. Grouping notes and rests. Transposition at the octave.
More than two ledger lines.
Writing four-bar rhythms. Anacrusis. Phrases.
More musical terms and signs.

ISBN 1-898771-00-6

THEORY IS FUN GRADE 4

All key signatures to 5 sharps or 5 flats. Alto clef; chromatic scale, double sharps and flats. Technical names of notes in the diatonic scale. Simple and compound time: duple, triple, quadruple. Primary triads: tonic, subdominant and dominant. All diatonic intervals up to an octave. Recognising ornaments. Four-bar rhythms and rhythms to words.
Families of orchestral instruments and their clefs.
More musical terms, including French.

ISBN 1-898771-01-4

THEORY IS FUN GRADE 5

All key signatures to 7 sharps or 7 flats. Tenor clef and scales. Compound intervals: major, minor, perfect, diminished and augmented. Irregular time signatures: quintuple and septuple. Tonic, supertonic, subdominant and dominant chords.
Writing at concert pitch. Short and open score. Orchestral instruments in detail. Composing a melody for instrument or voice. Perfect, imperfect and plagal cadences.
More musical terms, including German.

ISBN 0-9516940-9-X